MEN-AT-ARMS SE

EDITOR: PHILIP WARNER

Japanese Army of World War II

Text by PHILIP WARNER

Colour plates by MICHAEL YOUENS

OSPREY PUBLISHING LIMITED

Published in 1973 by
Osprey Publishing Ltd, P.O. Box 25,
707 Oxford Road, Reading, Berkshire
© Copyright 1973 Osprey Publishing Ltd

ISBN 0 85045 118 3

Printed in Great Britain.
Monochrome by BAS Printers Limited,
Wallop, Hampshire
Colour by Colour Reproductions Ltd., Billericay.

The Japanese Concept of War

The Japanese Army, between 1939 and 1945, was divided into two main sections: the Fighting and the Service branches. However, the division did not exactly correspond with that between fighting arms and services in other armies.

The *Heika*, or line branch, included infantry, cavalry, artillery, engineers, air service and transport. The *Kabuku*, or services branch, included medical, veterinary, and clerical services. In the *Heika*, personnel could readily be transferred from one unit to another; in the *Kabuku*, this was not so, except for relatively unskilled lower ranks. In addition there was a third branch – the *Kempei* (Military Police). The *Kempei* had originally been classified as part of an arm but, as the Japanese Empire expanded, it took on a virtually independent role. No Japanese soldier, nor for that matter anyone else, would ever wish to attract the attention of the *Kempei*.

RANKS AND DISCIPLINE

The ranks in the Japanese Army corresponded closely with ranks in the Allied Powers, but their powers and authority were different. *Gensui* (Field-Marshal) was the highest rank, but it was a title rather than a functional appointment. It would be granted by the Emperor to a general deserving of special honour. Senior or successful generals might therefore receive this title without varying their command.

An army was commanded by a general, but in the Japanese organization an army was equivalent in size to a corps in the British or American armies. The *Taisho* (General) therefore held equivalent command to an Allied lieutenant-general, who would of course usually, though not invariably, be a corps commander. The *Chujo* (Lieutenant-General) commanded a division, and was therefore equal in status to an Allied major-general. The *Shōshō* (Major-General) commanded a brigade, or sometimes an infantry group. The rank of brigadier did not exist in the Japanese military hierarchy. His function was sometimes covered by the *Shōshō* (Major-General), but more often by the *Taisa* (Colonel). The *Taisa* commanded a regiment consisting of three battalions, each of which was commanded by a *Shōsa* (Major). The *Taisa* therefore usually had three *Shōsas* responsible to him, but he also had a second-in-command, a *Chūsa* (equivalent to Lieutenant-Colonel) to assist

Men of the 1st Imperial Guard Infantry Regiment in peaked service caps and M90 uniform, introduced in 1930. Note the special Guards cap-badge, the rank bars worn on the shoulder, the red collar tabs with yellow metal regimental numbers, and the characteristic outward 'sag' of the heavy ammunition pouches

Japanese officer in 1930 uniform, with field cap. Note that the rank bars on each shoulder have been removed for security reasons. The belt is of stiched fabric, for field wear. The cross-straps support equipment worn on the hips or behind the body, such as pistol holster, map-case, binocular case, and gas-mask bag. The sword was often carried in action, both as a traditional symbol of authority and as a weapon. (Imperial War Museum)

him. This was a compact system of command, though some might find it too sparse. At battalion level the pattern became closer to the Allied system. A company was commanded by a *Tai-i* (Captain); a platoon was commanded by a *Chū-i* (1st Lieutenant) or a *Shō-i* (2nd Lieutenant). A *Jun-i* was the equivalent of a Regimental Sergeant-Major; and a *Socho*, of a Company Sergeant-Major. A *Gunsō* (Sergeant) was platoon sergeant and a *Gochō* (Corporal) was a section leader. A *Heichō* was a Lance-Corporal, and private soldiers were in three categories: *Jōtōhei* (senior), *Ittōhei* (first class) and *Nitōhei* (second class). But the authority conferred by one rank over another was vastly greater than in the British or American armies.

Pay was much lower than in the Allied armies,

possibly because of the much lower standard and cost of living in Japan. It varied between the General's pay of 550 yen a month and the second-class private's pay of 6 yen a month, the value of the yen at that time being approximately 6p. All this must of course be seen in relation to the prevailing pattern of Japanese life and army life in particular. The soldier had his clothing provided for him and he looked after it with meticulous care, as far as conditions allowed. If he could not make someone else sew up a tear, or put on a patch, he would do so himself – and very neatly. Although by no means smart in appearance, the Japanese soldier usually looked fairly neat. Officers managed to preserve a tidy appearance even in the field. Normal civilian clothing closely resembled that of the soldier, and puttees would be worn wrapped around their legs to knee height in order to save wear – the transition from civilian to soldier in uniform was not therefore the large step that it was in other countries.

Food, whether at home or in the field differed little, if at all. The combatant soldier carried a supply of rice which he could boil up in his kidney-shaped mess tin and supplement with a little dried fish or beans. If any form of unit cooking was possible he would have some sort of stew, usually based on soya-bean sauce. Given the chance, he would supplement his diet with what he could acquire: chicken, pork, vegetables, fruit and a little *sake* (rice beer). These latter delights were infrequent, and it was found that when the Japanese Army was on the path of conquest, considerable discomfort and sickness was brought on by indulgence in rich and unfamiliar foods. Sickness, of course, made no difference to what was expected of a Japanese soldier. It was virtually a crime to be sick, and the soldier himself felt it to be a disgrace. When, therefore, the jungle diseases began to take their toll the average Japanese felt that in some obscure way it was his own fault – a view reinforced by his being told, 'Sick men do not need food; if they cannot work or fight they should not eat.' With all this went a tremendous sense of dedication which had been hammered into him from his earliest years. And even if his own dedication was of a less exalted kind than that of his senior officers, it made no difference; he was so utterly subservient to authority – which he would never dream of questioning – that he did what was expected of him and more. The final proof of the Japanese soldier's dedication was shown when the enemy was nearing his homeland, and no one could ask for better proof than that displayed in the defence of Iwo Jima and Okinawa.

DEDICATION TO DEATH

The spiritual drive of the Japanese soldier is something not easily understood by the modern Westerner, although something closely akin to it has been found in many other nations in history. As a son of Japan, he sees his highest fulfilment in death on the battlefield. This achieves all he can desire. Not only is he dying for the Emperor, the Son of Heaven, but more than that he will himself become a god, a part of the universal soul. Small wonder that he will run straight at a machine-gun as if it is not there, that he will hold a position till nothing short of a flame-thrower will clear it, that he will launch himself suicidally as a kamikaze pilot. Nor is it easy for him to see that there are other ways of fighting wars, and that endless sacrifice of human life and effort does not always bring success.

The iron discipline of the Japanese soldier has a curious background: it is based on organization and certain deeply held beliefs. First among these is the belief that just as there is a rigid hierarchical society in Japan, with the Emperor at the head, so the world, too, has a natural hierarchy of which

Japanese troops in winter dress during the early stages of the Sino-Japanese War, with a 1914, Model 3, 6·5 mm. heavy machine-gun mounted on a carrying frame. Note particularly the old-style steel helmets with their pronounced 'brim', worn over a woollen toque in cold weather. (Imperial War Museum)

Japan is the proper head. The fact that this particular order of nations is not yet established in no way deters the Japanese from believing in it. It is of course considerably easier to believe that your mission will be successful if you think it is divinely ordained than if you think of it merely as a worthwhile venture. The same attitude – and the same success – may be found in many revolutionary movements – indeed in Christianity itself. 'Blessed are the meek, for they shall inherit the earth.' The Japanese were anything but meek, but they held the same inner conviction as Christians, that ultimately, despite all set-backs, their cause would triumph.

This dedication had some curious results. The tremendous fighting spirit of the Japanese already referred to is obviously one of them. Another is the kamikaze spirit which caused Japanese pilots to crash their suicide planes on to ships, or to man midget submarines which were a form of guided torpedo. A less obvious result was what might seem the absurd orthodoxy of certain Japanese convictions. Foreigners in Japan in 1944 were surprised to see Japanese factory workers doing energetic physical jerks in squads at intervals during the day. Considering the food shortage it seemed that they might have done better to conserve their energy. But this was not the way the Japanese thought of it. Even a sick person would benefit from physical exercises if he or she had the right spirit.

One consequence of this outlook was that actions which were regarded as absurd by Westerners were acceptable to the Japanese. The sword would be carried almost everywhere, even though its uses in modern warfare are naturally limited. Japanese pilots would carry swords even in aircraft. One extraordinary story put out by the *Syonan Times*, a newspaper printed in English for the English-speaking peoples of Singapore, recorded that a pilot, having dropped all his bombs and fired all his guns, dived at a battleship and, as he passed the bridge, cut off an officer's head with his sword. This story, printed at an early stage in the war, seemed to Westerners merely absurd; later, when pilots were crashing their planes on battleships, with samurai swords in the cockpits, the story seemed less ridiculous; not that it seemed any more likely, but because it was entirely

Crew of a Model 94 75 mm. pack gun. Note variations in clothing and headgear. The officer on the right wears the second-pattern sun helmet; the yellow artillery tabs on the collar of the 1930 tunic are clearly visible. (Imperial War Museum)

credible to the Japanese themselves and was typical of their dedicated approach.

CODE OF CONDUCT

Any sign of backsliding by a Japanese soldier was of course promptly dealt with by his superiors. Furthermore, his resolve was stimulated by the regular reading of the Imperial Rescript. The Imperial Rescript, issued in 1882 by the Emperor Meji, was read on national holidays, and certain other prescribed days, and members of the armed forces were required to learn it. It emphasized the duty owed by the Japanese serviceman to the Emperor and to the national and military system, and the supreme importance of courage, frugality and single-mindedness.

The Japanese soldier's dedication to his ideals includes *bushido*. This may be described as the way of the samurai (the warrior class) and was a code of Japanese chivalry. It extolled the virtues of courage, benevolence, politeness, loyalty and self-control. Allied prisoners of war were unable to believe that such a code could ever exist among their captors, but it must be borne in mind that the whole idea of respect for the prisoner of war was completely alien to the Japanese way of thinking. And, of course, it must not be overlooked that the treatment of Allied prisoners of war was not greatly different from the Japanese soldier's treatment of his fellow soldier. They themselves were herded together, were hard-worked and were punished with or without reason. The concept of maintaining the troops' morale with books, letters, concerts and home leave was simply unknown in the Japanese Army. Periodically soldiers would be given a little luxury, in the form of *sake* or an extra ration of fish; not, however, in order to boost morale but only as reward. There was no need to give rewards of course; a man did his utmost and beyond it, without any thought of personal gain.

To the soldier of any other army Japanese discipline would seem incredible; to those of their adversaries unfortunate enough to be captured it became only too familiar. Its simplest form was face-slapping. This is a time-honoured Japanese custom, by no means the joke that it is in the West. It could happen at almost any level but, needless to say, it was most prevalent among the lower ranks. A second-year soldier walking past a group of first-year soldiers might decide that he had not been saluted promptly enough. (All ranks are saluted.) He would line them up and walk along the line slapping each one hard across the face as they stood rigidly to attention. Then, in all probability, he would walk up and down again several times, slapping as he went. A few might be knocked over by the force of the blows but they would rise hastily to their feet and resume the position of attention. He might perhaps leave it at that; or he might let them stand there in the sun for some time; or again he might get worked up and punch them by way of variation. An officer who felt affronted might give a man a blow across the face with the flat of his sword. At certain times, in the case of a more serious offence, such as slowness or lateness, the punisher would use some suitable weapon at hand. It might be a stick or a rifle-butt. But this was nothing to what a man would get if he fell foul of the *Kempei*. Then he would be battered into unconsciousness, and be kicked as he lay. When he revived he would be knocked down again; and that might be only the beginning. Often the soldier might not know why he was being punished. Sometimes after a severe beating he might be astonished to receive a bowl of rice or a cigarette from his beater. The reason why was never explained. To explain would be to lose face.

All this was doubtless good for discipline. A man would learn to take a blow without flinching, and to be constantly alert. It did not seem to stifle initiative, and as a regular practice it was never questioned. The Japanese, in the Army or out of it, are accustomed to wielding or submitting to authority. Politeness and deference are instilled from birth. The bowing is endless, and even a bow has its grades and variations. Extreme politeness and deference might be shown by hissing slightly as one spoke. Politeness is even applied to objects. The prefix 'o' denoting 'honourable' is applied to such words as 'cha' (= tea), which will be referred to as 'o-cha' (= honourable tea). Other words so formed often referred to deified objects in ancient Japan: 'o-tenki' = the weather, 'o-yu' = hot water, 'o-kane' = money. A similar survival in the English language is the name given to weekdays: Tiw's day, Woden's day, Thor's day, Frig's day. 'O' is, however, more frequently applied to people. O

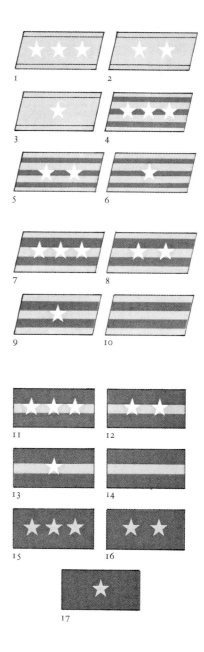

Rank insignia – officers (Nos. 1–10): 1 Taisho (General); 2 Chujo (Lieutenant-General); 3 Shōshō (Major-General); 4 Taisa (Colonel); 5 Chūsa (Lieutenant-Colonel); 6 Shōsa (Major); 7 Tai-i (Captain); 8 Chū-i (1st Lieutenant); 9 Shō-i (2nd Lieutenant); 10 Jūn-i (Warrant Officer)
Rank insigna – non-commissioned officers and enlisted men (Nos. 11–19): 11 Socho (Sergeant-Major); 12 Gunso (Sergeant); 13 Gochō (Corporal); 14 Heichō (Lance-Corporal); 15 Jōtōhei (Senior Private); 16 Ittōhei (Private 1st Class,); 17 Nitōhei (Private, 2nd Class)
Insignia for all ranks of general consisted of white stars on a yellow background; for colonels and major, white stars over dull red stripes on a yellow background; for captains, lieutenants and warrant officers, white stars over a yellow line on a red background edged with yellow; for N.C.O.s, white stars over a yellow line on a dull red background, and for privates, yellow stars on a dull red background

7

This photograph of General Sugiyama illustrates the turn-down collar and new rank patches of the 1938 tunic. (Imperial War Museum)

Hara San = Miss Blossom, O Matsu San = Miss Pine-tree.

There were, of course, many features of Japanese life, inside and outside the Army, which were incomprehensible and often inconceivable to their opponents. Because of their system the Japanese made superb fighting soldiers, but also because of their system their discipline could be disrupted. But it must not be thought that the individual Japanese lacked initiative nor that he would collapse when isolated. On numerous occasions a Japanese, perhaps wounded, would be lying in hiding, and then after a day or two without food would try to inflict some damage on Allied troops. Even now Japanese soldiers who lost contact with their units in World War II occasionally turn up from remote jungle-covered islands, believing that the war is still continuing. Many Japanese soldiers were told that the war might last for twenty or thirty or even a hundred years, and were prepared to fight that long.

The ideal death was, of course, death in battle in a moment of victory. But, as the Japanese knew, there could be other occasions than victory. There could be moments of defeat when the alternatives would be death or disgrace. At that point the son of Nippon (Japan) would know what to do. He must commit *hara-kiri*, the ceremonial suicide which a man chose in preference to dishonour. At the end of World War II General Tojo attempted to commit *hara-kiri*; this form of suicide still happens occasionally. Originally it was done by disembowelling oneself. *Hara-kiri* means literally 'to cut the stomach'. Recently the disembowelling became more of a ceremonial act; a man would make, as it were, a 'token' slit across his stomach before putting a revolver to his head. There are many countries in which a person who feels himself disgraced or without hope will commit suicide; but it is unusual to make a ceremonial act of it.

Japanese culture is a mystery to most Westerners; and perhaps also to many Japanese. All countries are an amalgam of many influences but to few has it fallen to be so isolated and yet so heavily influenced as Japan. The Japanese islands are not rich or fertile; it has therefore been necessary for this people to work extremely hard for very little, to live at close quarters, and to develop a way of life which made their existence tolerable. The Japanese are small and wiry because they have little food but plenty of work; they are polite because when you live at close quarters politeness is not merely a virtue but a necessity. For two hundred years Japan was completely isolated from the Western world, and its population was kept under check by abortion and infanticide. Having made contact with the outside world since the middle of the nineteenth century, and being totally unable to feed its rapidly rising population, Japan had to expand in order to survive.

All this is easily understandable. However, during its period of imperial conquest, in China, in Malaya, in Burma, in the Philippines and elsewhere in the Pacific, the Japanese committed atrocities which were anything but cultured or civilized. Such things were inconceivable to Westerners until an account of them emerged in the book written by Lord Russell of Liverpool, *The Knights of Bushido* (published by Cassell in 1958), based on the evidence of the war crimes trials. The book is too gruesome to be widely read, but one of its most significant pictures shows Japanese soldiers who had been bayoneted to death by other Japanese as their army was retreating. The dead men were all sick or wounded in a Japanese hospital on the Philippine island of Luzon; they were killed to prevent their being captured alive. Doubtless their killers thought they were 'saving face' for them. But anyone who lived in a country occupied by the Japanese between 1941 and 1945 would never be surprised at any deed committed by them.

Nevertheless, to imagine that all Japanese soldiers went around committing atrocities would be utterly wrong. Many, in the bewildering circumstances in which they found themselves, behaved much better than might have been expected. Moreover, most of those responsible for hideous atrocities and cruelty received their deserts from the War Crimes Commission. Japan, as a nation, has paid an appalling price at home for its soldiers' misdeeds overseas.

How the Japanese Army fought

In 1941 the Allies were caught unprepared by the Japanese Army. As late as 1940 the author was told, 'The Japanese are no good, they have no aircraft and no good weapons, and when it rains they call off a battle and all go home.' Interesting words to recall when the Japanese were fighting like tigers in the monsoon rains in Burma.

Common sense should have told the Allies that the Japanese would be opponents to reckon with. They were known to be first-class at learning, at construction and at imitation. They were very

Group of infantry with company flags: China, 1938. Note field caps worn back to front – the steel helmet was often worn over the reversed cap. (Imperial War Museum)

good at obtaining intelligence; their photographers were everywhere. Equally, they were surprisingly good at concealing information about their own plans and resources.

TACTICS

By 1941 they had been fighting for ten years, ever since their first invasion and conquest of Manchuria, so necessary to them for raw materials. They had fought tank battles, they had made successful landings on many different kinds of territory, they had shown themselves to be successful in coping with conditions varying from jungle and open primitive country to urban areas and street fighting. In all these areas their principle had been: 'Maintain the offensive, move with great rapidity, keep the command well forward so that the utmost flexibility in orders is available, and keep all plans simple.' The assumption was that if any plan was carried through with enough speed and determination it would succeed. Even a defensive plan would embody the principle that the enemy was to be annihilated. By other armies an enemy probe might be contained, blunted, or even repulsed; by the Japanese it would be eliminated.

They would make use of surprise on all occasions, even at the sacrifice of preliminary reconnaissance. Japanese units would therefore often attack superior forces, partly to achieve confidence, partly because they believed that a superior force could be put into disorder by a totally unexpected attack. At times the experiment cost them dear.

Deep infiltration was also a part of their tactical doctrine. The effect of a few enemy soldiers in one's rear is invariably damaging to morale. In the early days of their imperial conquest some Japanese hurled themselves at strongpoints, others flowed around them. They would seize bicycles, boats or civilian transport, and penetrate by narrow jungle paths. The Allies, knowing that armies cannot move in any strength through trackless country, but need roads to bring up supplies, ammunition and reinforcements, decided that jungle and swamp would be a sufficient bar to the Japanese. They soon found out their mistake. Although a dozen Japanese soldiers on bicycles cannot conquer an area, they can do

considerable damage if they burst unsuspected on to a headquarters. This is what happened in December 1941 to 6th Brigade H.Q. in northern Malaya. A small party of Japanese pressed through the jungle and caught H.Q. by surprise. All but two inside the building were killed within minutes. This technique of warfare is, however, only effective in a mobile situation or when the front lines are too long to be completely manned.

The value of the continued offensive was constantly stressed in Japanese Field Service Regulations and other textbooks. It was assumed that once troops came to close quarters the Japanese would be superior with rifle or bayonet, but with this went the conviction that the army which continued the offensive was always certain to win. In 1944, when Japanese forces had no option but to give ground, this belief was damaging to morale, although the average Japanese soldier seemed not to be greatly affected. Nevertheless the constant emphasis on attacking as often as possible cost the Japanese many casualties, since these attacks tended to neglect supporting arms and ignore the vital military doctrine of concentration of maximum force at the required time.

If possible, the Japanese always liked to envelop their opponents. This is a time-honoured manœuvre, to which Genghiz Khan's armies many centuries before had owed much of their success. The pattern, which soon became familiar to the Allies, was that the Japanese unit would advance in two columns (sometimes, but rarely, three). One or more columns would move along the enemy flank. A further column would engage the enemy frontally, and not allow it to disengage. The flanking column would then try to force its way round to the rear. It might perhaps be stronger than the column engaged in the frontal attack.

Another manœuvre was simply to advance until resistance was encountered, and while the main offensive appeared to the enemy to be concentrated at one point, large numbers would be detached from the Japanese main front (possibly leaving it with inferior numbers) and these detached units would begin an encircling movement, sometimes taking the form of a double pincer. If cut off, the Japanese soldier might engage in a suicide attack – which was the most

This picture captures a hint of the inexorable advance of the Japanese armies of 1941. The soldiers lead mules with a disassembled Model 41 75 mm. infantry gun; note the field caps with neck-cloths, the semi-breeches worn with puttees, and the characteristic rolled sleeves and white scarves. (Imperial War Museum)

satisfactory to his opponents for thus he would be identified and killed; but he might lie up in a hiding-place, perhaps in a tree, waiting for a chance to use his grenades to greatest effect.

These tactics, when successful, were highly effective; but when they failed, extremely costly. The Japanese were short of heavy artillery, and were not over-equipped with the tanks necessary to make a breach through a solid front. In consequence, if an offensive was checked, they would themselves be annihilated.

For training purposes the Japanese made much of what is called the 'meeting engagement'. This occurs when two forces, both advancing, meet each other and fight. Obviously, any victory gained at such a moment is likely to be decisive, even if only locally. The situation calls for immediate rapid action and flexibility and makes maximum demands on subordinate commanders.

A column varied considerably in strength but would normally include all or part of an infantry regiment, an anti-tank battalion, an engineer regiment (for building bridges and fortifications, making demolitions, etc.), an artillery regiment for 'softening-up' the target area, a decontamination unit, a casualty clearing unit, a howitzer regiment, a signals unit, transport elements and tanks.

When a division advanced towards a meeting engagement in two-column formation it would be preceded by a reconnaissance detachment, made up of light fast vehicles, or even infantry, which would be followed by tanks. The recce units would indicate suitable targets to tanks, which would try to shell them to pieces, or force a way through. As the columns approached the area, the left (or right) flanking column would advance level with the advance guard of the main column. The troops in each would include elements of those described above. Behind, but probably overlapping the rear of the flanking column, would come the main body, containing much more artillery. The unit as a whole would be commanded by the commander of the centre column, except that the reconnaissance element of the flanking column would not come under direct command from the main body but only under its own column command. This might seem a little peculiar in that a flanking column might well run into situations where its operations should probably be under a main rather than a detachment commander. It should be remembered that the advance parties designated by the Japanese were very strong, far stronger than the Allied advance parties. But then their function and use was different. And it is scarcely necessary to add that the road network, and the nature of the terrain, made a difference to the exact deployment of troops, though the columns would generally be about twenty miles apart.

A battalion normally had a frontage of 1,600 yards, and a regiment held approximately three times this area, although the regimental strength might be more concentrated, e.g. two battalions in first-line attacks, and one in reserve if the situation justified this deployment. Aircraft and artillery were required to give close support if needed – and if they happened to be available for the purpose. When attacking, Japanese divisions did not attempt to maintain alignment, and as a result were open to counter-infiltration which might engage artillery units following up for close support. Tactically some of their methods would have been suicidal had not all troops, even those in support units, been infected with the same dedicated idealism as the forward troops. But, even with that asset, set-back often turned to disaster. Their tactical doctrine thus frequently produced over-confidence in situations which did not justify it.

When warfare settled down, and the enemy held various strong positions, the Japanese tactic was to try to turn them or to approach under conditions of surprise. This might be done either by night attack, although here the Japanese could find themselves even more at a disadvantage, or in bad weather, when visibility might be very low, or from a direction which might be thought impossible owing to the terrain. It was always believed that if everything was committed, with the added element of surprise, success was assured. The

A British soldier being searched by his Japanese captors. The slightly scruffy appearance and individual disposition of kit displayed by the soldier on the right is typical of the Japanese infantryman in the field. (Imperial War Museum)

attack would be maintained continuously, so long as there was anything or anyone to maintain it. Its cessation meant that for the time being resources in that area were exhausted.

Once the Allies appreciated the strength and weakness of these tactics, Japanese losses were very high. These were often caused by insufficient preparation and the lack or misuse of artillery. To attack a well-defended, well-wired position without adequate artillery preparation is to ask for casualties, but this apparently did not deter the Japanese, who seemed to expect to pay a high price.

Nevertheless, Japanese tactics frequently gave them tremendous advantages. In open country, where resistance was not well co-ordinated, their ability to follow up a victory often shortened a campaign by months. In China, especially, the Japanese followed up with great speed on foot, in captured transport and on railways. The Japanese believed that one of their greatest skills was night attack, and would therefore employ it on targets which they would not consider vulnerable in daylight. It offered them an opportunity to get to close quarters and avoid accurate enemy fire which would have made advance impossible in daylight. Night attacks, however, were used in a variety of ways. They were launched when a division was retiring but wished to conceal the intention of the main body; they were used to maintain an offensive and prevent opponents from getting any respite; and they were valuable psychologically. Even if a night attack took place on only one night in five the other nights could be made unpleasant for the enemy by a few men blowing bugles in the jungle or making threats through a loud-hailer. To new troops this could be a serious menace, though it might be taken later as a joke. For preference the Japanese organized night attacks to take place between midnight and 2 a.m. Later in World War II Japanese tactics had to be varied considerably, for the orthodoxy and offensive spirit of their night operations led them straight to well-prepared Allied positions and consequently heavy losses.

Not surprisingly, the Japanese Army disliked defensive tactics and therefore tended to neglect them in training. Like other armies, however, they had a formal defensive arrangement creating zones of automatic fire and anti-tank obstacles. Defensive fire would normally be echeloned to give a herring-bone fire-pattern. Nevertheless, the defensive was so unpopular that soldiers were always apt to leap out of their positions and meet the oncoming enemy with bayonets. On few occasions did this provide anything but the most temporary gain. In the later stages of the war, when the Army was holding island positions, the Japanese soldier would wait till the last possible moment before emerging to use his bayonet or grenade. On Okinawa, as in many other places, their discipline and determination were so great that the Americans would approach foxholes warily with flame-throwers; even then some Japanese soldiers stayed in their positions.

An officer with leather buckled leggings, slung sword and binocular-case watches his rifle squad advance along a railway embankment. Note that these troops wear hessian helmet-covers, and are in shirt-sleeve order. (Imperial War Museum)

ARMAMENT

So far, we have mainly discussed the role of the infantry. The Japanese were, however, fully alert to the potentialities of mechanical forces, as the Allies soon learnt. The use they made of tanks was normally as an infantry support weapon.

Their tanks fell into four main groups:

1. the tankette – under 5 tons;
2. the light tank – under 10 tons;
3. the medium tank – under 20 tons;
4. the heavy tank – over 20 tons.

Clearly, these changed considerably both in design and armament during the war. Initially they were fitted with low-velocity 37 mm. and 57 mm. guns, which were later replaced with high-velocity models. Most of them also carried machine-guns fitted with an armoured protector. The armour itself was normally light but of high quality. Tank design was also good, giving the maximum possible area for deflection of attacking fire. They were fitted with diesel engines, which probably owed much to German advice. Usually they had a combination of vision slits and periscopes. Not surprisingly there was little provision for escape hatches; perhaps it was felt that a tank crew should die with their tank just as a good captain goes down with his ship. On the same thinking it was notable that Japanese tanks tended to have high power, good firepower, and speed achieved by the reduction of the weight of armaments to the minimum. Included in the tanks' firepower were flame-throwers, but these were not used until late in the war. Early tanks had considerable problems from internal fumes but later designs eliminated most of these drawbacks.

THE TANKETTE. Of the types outlined above the tankette was one of the most continuously operational. It had a height of 5 ft. 4 in., a width of 5 ft. 3 in. and was 11 ft. long. With a turret at the rear it looked not unlike a mobile boot. It had a two-man crew, and (usually) a 7·7 mm. machine-gun mounted on the turret. Its speed was 25 miles an hour and it had a range of 100 miles. Naturally these vehicles were often used as personnel carriers over short distances. Suspension of all models was the Carden-Lloyd type.

The Japanese made no great use of tanks in the later stages of the war, but they saw service in China and in the initial invasions of 1941. This is a 10-ton light tank, Model 95 Ha-Go; it has a crew of three, and the main armament is of 37 mm. calibre. (Imperial War Museum)

THE LIGHT TANK. The average light tank weighed just under 8 tons. It was 6 ft. high, 5 ft. 11 in. wide and just under 15 ft. long. It carried a three-man crew and had armour approximately twice the thickness of that on the tankette (22 mm. as opposed to 12 mm.). Some light tanks had six-cylinder air-cooled 85 h.p. petrol engines. (This was about 30 h.p. more powerful than that fitted in the tankette.) They had a small, round, tapered turret with a machine-gun mounted on it, and often a machine-gun also mounted at the rear.

Other light tanks, especially the 95, a mass-produced tank of pre-war design which saw the Japanese through the first half of the war, had diesel engines. The 95 tank developed up to 110 h.p. and carried a 37 mm. gun in addition to two machine-guns. The turret gunner was the tank commander. Although the turret would traverse through 360 degrees it was manually operated. Very few of these tanks were equipped with radio, and the tank commander had to use a speaking-tube to communicate with the driver, and flags to signal to other tanks. The weakness of the firepower of this tank was that the gun could be elevated only 24 degrees and depressed only 20 degrees from the horizontal. However, as protection against people wishing to 'investigate' the tank by getting under the lowest gun depression and then lobbing a grenade into the turret, the tank commander carried his own supply of grenades. The machine-guns had a slightly wider arc of fire but not complete enough to make the tank, when closed up, completely self-protective. Some tanks therefore had an average area of 20 ft. in all directions from the sides which was complete 'dead space' as far as their guns were concerned. Anyone lying up unobserved who had a tank within that range could use an anti-tank gun with virtual impunity.

THE MEDIUM TANK. There was, predictably, a wide variety of these useful tanks, but the general characteristic was a weight of 15 tons, a length of 18 ft., a width of $7\frac{1}{2}$ ft., and a height of nearly 8 ft. They carried a crew of four men and had armour of varying thickness. At the front and sides of the hull the armour was up to 26 mm. thick, but on the lower side was seldom more than 9 mm.

Medium tanks had a crew of four, and in later models carried a 47 mm. high-velocity tank gun as well as 7·7 mm. machine-guns front and rear. Most of these tanks were equipped with smoke-generator dischargers capable of launching canisters to 50 yards. They would carry 120 rounds of 47 mm. ammunition and up to 4,000 rounds of 7·7 mm. machine-gun ammunition.

The speed of the later medium tanks did not vary significantly from that of the earlier versions, being about 25 m.p.h. (Discussions on the merits of speed versus armament and firepower never cease in military circles, no matter which the nation. The ideal is a tank which can travel reasonably fast, yet leave its occupants in condition to use concentrated firepower, all the while being protected from anti-tank fire by the resistance of their armour. Added to this may be the requirement to climb and descend steep gradients and, if necessary, act as a static strongpoint.)

THE HEAVY TANK. The Japanese had few heavy tanks, probably because the terrain and type of fighting rarely called for them. A heavy tank, when fully active, is an awesome piece of equipment, but its disadvantages are also considerable. It has inevitably a fairly low speed, and it cannot traverse ground negotiable by lighter-armoured vehicles. The heaviness of the armament makes its component parts, such as brakes, very liable to overheating. In tropical or sub-tropical conditions all tanks tend to become overheated, and the wear and tear on tank crews cannot be ignored. The Japanese 'heavy' tank was one of 30 tons, a weight which in the European theatre would probably have been classed as medium or even light. The advantage of the Japanese 'heavy', however, was that it could bring larger-calibre guns to the vital areas. In addition to the armament on the medium tank, it had a 75 mm. gun.

THE AMPHIBIOUS TANK. In addition to the above, the Japanese had, of course, amphibious tanks. The latter are equipped with front and rear pontoons, enabling them to float, and propellers to move them along when waterborne. Once on land, they shed the pontoons and differ little from a normal land tank. There are of course seals to keep water from seeping in when used amphibiously, and these close all openings up to the turret-ring.

For reconnaissance the Japanese had a variety of armoured cars. Their performance varied considerably. Most of them had a speed of 40–50 m.p.h. and were lightly armoured; but they carried four men and five machine-guns. Some were made easily convertible to run on railway lines, but these usually had solid rubber tyres when on the road. The conversion to or from flanged wheels was made in ten minutes. One reason why the Japanese showed little uniformity in their armoured cars was that after they had once overrun huge areas they had their pick of a variety of transport, some of which could be converted. Although many vehicles were immobilized or damaged by retreating troops the Japanese were skilled at getting them on the move again. Eventually the only limiting factor was fuel, for though the Japanese captured considerable quantities of oil its distribution became extremely difficult as the war in the Pacific progressed.

Before leaving armoured vehicles we must take a look at self-propelled guns. These were naturally very close in design to tanks but needed certain variations. The gun was usually virtually identical with the wheeled gun, but the tank turret clearly required considerable modification. The gun itself was given a traverse of 20 degrees and an elevation range from −5 to +25 degrees.

USE OF ARMOURED FIGHTING VEHICLES

Although initially thought by the Allies to be a somewhat primitive and unmechanized army, the Japanese soon showed that they were fully aware of the value of mechanization. An example was quickly provided in Malaya which the Allies thought was not 'tank country', and therefore had only a limited number of bren-gun carriers there. The Japanese not only introduced tanks but also employed them successfully in areas which were thought to be totally unsuitable. The effect of the appearance of a tank, followed by another tank, in an area to which it is thought they could not penetrate can have an effect far beyond the firepower of the vehicle itself. Furthermore a suitable welcome will not have been established. Nevertheless, even with their appreciation of the armoured fighting vehicle and success in its use,

it is doubtful whether the Japanese ever had the time or the opportunity to work out the full possibilities of tank tactics.

In December 1941 when the Japanese simultaneously attacked Pearl Harbor, Hong Kong and Malaya, they had four tank regiments. These were enough for the purpose; later, Burma required more, and this, with their long line of communication, proved a major logistical problem.

As a general rule, tank squadrons remained independent, and therefore, in theory, could be attached to the unit whose need was greatest at any given time. This clearly required close support from the infantry. The role of armoured units, however, is not merely to support other arms but to destroy opposed armoured units.

In the Pacific fighting zone there was little open country and no broad stretches of desert of the type suited to large armoured formations. Had the Japanese succeeded in breaking through into India

Typical of the improvisation which took the Japanese soldier and his equipment through 'impassable' jungle – a living bridge across a Malayan river. (Imperial War Museum)

they would have encountered very different terrain and would doubtless have adapted themselves to it.

Japanese tank training, as in other arms, stressed the virtues of attack to the point of obsession. In consequence, having arrived swiftly and often secretly, but finding themselves held up by a well-defined obstacle, tank crews would abandon the vehicle and launch themselves into the assault as infantry shock troops. This procedure, although an admirable example of offensive spirit, often meant the elimination of specialized personnel who were not easily replaced. Japanese tank crews were highly trained to fight at night and in extremely bad weather; this type of training is neither rapid nor easy.

Japanese tank units had gained considerable experience in China but, since much of this was against poorly armed troops, it proved in the long run more of a drawback than an asset. Subsequently, when they met efficient and well-directed anti-tank fire they suffered higher losses through recklessness than was normal in such engagements.

The conventional pattern of a Japanese tank offensive was to hold the tanks in reserve until appropriate targets had been identified. Then, all being well, the tanks made a break-through and, if necessary, held ground by acting as a battery. If the situation required, tanks would assist in pursuit, breaking down any points of local resistance.

The soldier in the background is firing the standard Japanese light machine-gun at the outset of the war, the 1922, Model 11, gas-operated air-cooled gun of 6·5 mm. calibre. It only operated correctly with reduced-charge rifle cartridges, six clips of five rounds each being fed into the open hopper on the left side of the breech. (Imperial War Museum)

WEAPONS

There is unfortunately no space here to give a complete description of the wide variety of weapons employed by the Japanese, ranging from primitive rock mounds under water (to inflict damage upon landing-craft) to highly sophisticated rockets. In certain forms of equipment the Japanese were vastly inferior to their opponents, but in others they could match or outclass them. All Japanese optical instruments were of the highest quality, and sturdy as well. In 1941 the Allies assumed that Japanese artillery fire and bombing would be of low efficiency; but the accuracy of their high-altitude bombing and their success in sinking the *Prince of Wales* and the *Repulse* led to drastic modification of these views.

The Japanese also had a variety of weapons which only came into use later in the war. Some, such as piloted suicide aircraft, have been already mentioned. Others, when they were encountered, came as a surprise to the Allies. Among them were the flame-throwing tanks captured on Luzon. These carried up to five flame-throwers and two machine-guns, and also had iron forks at the front for clearing obstacles. Their speed was 25 m.p.h. Flame-throwing tanks had existed in the Japanese Army since before the war, but these later models showed very marked modification in design.

Like all armies, the Japanese had a wide variety of small arms, weapons, and equipment. But their pistols and sub-machine-guns, and their light, medium and heavy machine-guns were not substantially different from the Western types. Indeed the Japanese infantry soldier used a wide variety of captured Western army weapons without difficulty. They included Madsen light machine-guns captured from the Dutch. These are of Danish manufacture but had been supplied to the Dutch Army in the East Indies (Indonesia). There was a sprinkling of bren-guns. Brens were a very efficient type of light machine-gun of Czech design, which had a range of 2,000 yds. if needed, but were usually used at much less. The Japanese also used American M1 rifles and M1917 Enfield rifles. They had some Dutch Manlicher rifles and carbines and some Czech Mauser rifles.

MORTARS. To the infantryman on the ground one of the most impressive features of the Japanese was their skill with grenades and mortars. Some of these were highly sophisticated weapons, others were improvised from local materials. Both grenade-launchers and mortars are at a premium in rugged terrain where visibility is limited; and there are few experiences more irritating than to discover that a good defensive position, with excellent observation, is suddenly being peppered with extremely accurate mortar-fire.

The grenade-discharger is an extremely simple weapon consisting of little more than a tube and a base plate, and weighing 5–6 lb. The grenade is launched from the tube to the required range at the rate of some twenty rounds a minute. It can contain high-explosive, anti-personnel material, or incendiary matter. The classic grenade is the 36, known in World War I as the Mills bomb. This is usually thrown with a bowling action like a cricket ball. It is an ideal weapon for lobbing over obstacles, into doorways where it is thought the enemy are waiting, or into suspected ambush positions. It has a four-second fuse, just adequate for it to reach its target before exploding but insufficient for any brave man to pick it up and throw it back.

A grenade discharged from a launcher or rifle has a much greater range, of up to 1,000 yds. The base plate of the launcher was curved so that it could be put on any natural surface such as a tree trunk or rock. Launchers could discharge heavy grenades, weighing around 10 lb. Hand-grenades usually weighed about 1½ lb.

Mortars, although not usually considered accurate weapons, seemed to become so in the hands of the Japanese; this was probably because of intelligent guesswork and incessant practice.

Mortar bombs were approximately the size of their Allied counterparts (e.g. the 2 in., 3 in., and 4·2 in.), being 50 mm., 70 mm., 81 mm. and 150 mm. There was also in existence a 250 mm. spigot mortar which, though inaccurate, had a range of up to 1,500 yds. The projectile burst on a radius of 250 yds., and had, therefore, devastating effect against advancing troops.

The 81 mm. gave the Japanese excellent service in jungle warfare. It had a range of 2,000 yds., a total weight of 50 lb. and a short tube. It fired a 73·7 mm. shell containing H.E. Usually the shell exploded on impact, but it could be fused for air bursts if necessary.

These descriptions are very generalized, for the Japanese used a wide variety of weapons. Many of them were captured enemy equipment, since very large quantities of war materials had been dumped in areas which, in the imperfect strategy of the time, had been thought to be inaccessible to the Japanese. Fillings usually contained a considerable quantity of picric acid. The contents of a grenade naturally varied in accordance with its probable use, and those designed for tanks would need a vastly different mixture from those used against personnel.

MINES. Mines and booby traps are particularly hated by those exposed to them. Mines could take a variety of shapes from the shape of a frying-pan or kettle to that of a canvas bag or coconut. Attractive souvenirs were often booby-trapped. It was not uncommon for an explosive to be placed under a dead body; when the body was moved for burial or some other purpose the explosive would be activated. Coconuts were to be carefully avoided if the Japanese had been in occupation of the ground a short time before; when appropriately treated, they were not only effective against personnel within twenty yards but could also inflict considerable damage on small vehicles.

Beach mines, land mines and anti-tank mines were of the same principle as other mines but varied according to the setting for which they were designed. Mines such as these must be sown very thickly if the process is not to be wasteful. One of the most effective anti-tank mines was the 'pack' mine. This was a wooden box about twenty inches square, carried on the soldier's back, with an

Models of Baka piloted rocket glide bomb and the Navy twin-engined bomber, showing moment of release of the former

activation cord easily reached by the carrier. On seeing a tank approaching the soldier would remain concealed, but just as it came close enough would pull the cord and hurl himself between the tracks. The 'pack' mine was a characteristic Japanese suicide weapon.

ARTILLERY. Japanese artillery differed so little from basic Allied designs that it does not require detailed description. Outstanding were the 47 mm. anti-tank gun which had a muzzle velocity of 2·735 ft. per second with H.E. and was a most effective weapon, and a variety of 75 mm. guns including mountain guns which could be dismantled and made into six pack loads. There were also various types of howitzers, such as the type 99, 105 mm., which fired H.E.-pointed, H.E., and illuminating shells.

For coastal defence the Japanese used much larger weapons of the 120 mm. 45-calibre type. These had a range of 10,000–20,000 yds.

ROCKETS. Japanese rockets clearly owed much to German influence and experiment. Fortunately for the Allies they had not developed very far by 1945. Early ground-to-ground rockets were launched from a trough-shaped launcher. The range of these fairly simple weapons was 1,200 m. (1,311 yds.); later models, particularly the 20 cm. variety, were more efficient and were fairly accurate to 3,000 yds. The warhead weighed 86·3 lb. and contained 35·6 lb. of H.E. Larger but less accurate models included the 30 cm. fire-stabilized rocket which delivered a 435 lb. warhead to approximately 7,000 yds., and the 45 cm. Navy rocket which delivered 933 lb. to 2,000 yds. Suicide motor-boats carried two 120 mm. rockets loaded with a mixed charge which included a lot

The Baka piloted rocket glide bomb, right side view on dolly, with cockpit cover closed

of phosphorus pellets. They also included 560 lb. of conventional H.E.

GUIDED MISSILES. These are usually guided by remote control, but the Japanese had no difficulty in obtaining volunteers for this suicidal task. Their obvious use was against shipping, but they could also be employed against bombers or even ground depots. They were small, swept-wing monoplanes, with a range of 55 miles. They carried a warhead of some 2,500 lb.

PISTOLS. The standard Japanese pistols were the Nambu, the 14, and the 94, all of which were 8 mm. They had a few 9 mm., but these were neither successful nor reliable. The Nambu was a popular weapon. It was semi-automatic, recoil-operated and magazine-fed. The type 14 was meant to be an improvement, but it did not have the adjustable back sight of the Nambu. The 94 was a more compact design but had no other significant features. All three pistols were alleged to have a range of 50 yds. but, of course, revolvers are not accurate weapons, and are valued only for their stopping-power at short distances. The 9 mm. was quoted as having a range of 25 yds. only, but within that distance it had greater stopping-power than the others.

MACHINE-GUNS. The Japanese infantryman, with his marked ability for infiltration, was a deadly performer with a machine-gun, heavy or light. He

would often take a machine-gun where a man of another nation might have taken only a rifle. The effect of having a machine-gun spattering bullets on your rear or flank is considerable; nevertheless there is a marked limit to the amount of ammunition which can be carried and the effect is only temporary.

Japanese sub-machine-guns were 8 mm. fully automatic, with no provision for single-shot fire. The type-100 was fed from a 30-round box-type magazine mounted on the left (ejecting to the right). It was supported on a bipod, fitted with a bayonet, and could fire at the rate of 800 rounds a minute. The disadvantage of sub-machine-guns and light machine-guns is that they are not designed to be accurate weapons and they dispose of large quantities of heavy ammunition. They are ideal weapons for close-quarter work, but their weight, cumbrousness and extravagance in ammunition limits their usefulness.

The light machine-gun (l.m.g.) was 6·5 mm. and 7·7 mm. The type II feed consisted of six 5-round clips; these usually went through very smoothly because the feed mechanism incorporated an ammunition oiler. Its maximum effective range was 600 yds., and its effective rate of fire 120 rounds a minute, although the cyclic rate was 500 rounds a minute.

A subsequent version, the 96, also fired semi-rimmed 0·74 oz. ball ammunition but was able to dispense with the ammuniton oiler without loss of efficiency. It also had an efficient quick-change barrel, and some models had telescopic sights.

The type 99 had a few modifications, such as a more efficient barrel-locking device, and an adjustable monopod under the stock. The paratroop version had a detachable stock and a quick-change piston. The pistol grip was of steel (replacing wood). A serious drawback of these weapons was that parts of the 99 and 96, though identical in many ways, were not interchangeable: equally the semi-rimmed ammunition used in the heavy machine-guns could not be used in the l.m.g.s.

Heavy machine-guns (h.m.g.s) were of three calibres: 6·5 mm., 7·7 mm. and 13·2 mm.

The type 3 was gas-operated and air-cooled; it was mounted on a tripod and weighed, in all, 199 lb. It had a 28·63 in. barrel and was fed from 30-round strips. Its effective rate of fire was 150 rounds a minute.

The type 92, apart from its larger calibre, had other advantages, such as provision for mounting variable-power telescopic sights. It could also depress the firing rate by means of a gas regulator. It weighed 129 lb. (complete with carrying handles, tripod and telescopic sights). It had an effective rate of fire of 150 rounds a minute (450 cyclic) and a maximum effective range of 1,500 yds.

The type 1, 7·7 mm. h.m.g., was smaller than the 92, and thus about 50 per cent lighter. The barrel had been slightly modified to permit quicker changing. The overall length was 45·4 in., of which 23·2 was the barrel length. Its muzzle velocity was 2,400 ft. per second, its maximum effective range 1,500 yds., and its maximum rate of fire was 550 rounds a minute.

The type 92, 7·7 mm. (Lewis gun), was closely modelled on the British Lewis gun; it was used mainly by naval landing parties, but also by the Air Force and the Army. It was air-cooled, drum-fed and fired 7·7 mm. rimmed ammunition.

This gun had numerous useful features. Its maximum range was 4,500 yds., and it had a 360-degree traverse. It could fire up to 350 rounds a minute, and was fed from drum-type magazines holding 97 rounds.

The type 93, 13·2 mm., was primarily an anti-aircraft weapon but was also employed in ground fighting. Many ground-fighting weapons may be used for anti-aircraft firing but, if they are to be

The later and more sophisticated Model 99 weapon of 1939. The box magazine held thirty rounds of 7·7 mm. ammunition. Note the monopod pivoted on the heel of the butt. (Imperial War Museum)

effective, they need suitable sights and mounting. The type 93 had both pedestal and tripod mounts. It was gas-operated and air-cooled, and it incorporated a flash-hider on the muzzle. Its tracer range was 5,500 ft., its maximum effective slant range 3,000 ft. and its maximum horizontal range 5,500 yds. Its effective rate of fire was up to 350 rounds a minute. It had a 360-degree traverse and a 0–85-degree elevation. It was fed from a 30-round, box-type magazine.

ANTI-AIRCRAFT WEAPONS. One of the most effective and widely used Japanese anti-aircraft weapons was the 20 mm. machine cannon. It was used also against tanks. Gas-operated and air-cooled, it had a maximum effective slant range of 3,500 ft. and a maximum tracer range of 7,750 ft. Its horizontal range was 7,000 yds. It fired H.E. tracer, H.E. self-destroying tracer and anti-personnel tracer.

The 20 mm. cannon was eventually superseded by the 25 mm. cannon. This was primarily a Navy weapon, used extensively for anti-aircraft defence in the Pacific. It had twin barrels, each of which could fire 190 rounds a minute to an effective maximum slant range of 4,500 ft. Its horizontal range was 7,435 yds. It had a 360-degree traverse and a −10–85-degree elevation.

The Japanese used also a number of 40 mm. Vickers machine cannon (water-cooled, recoil-operated, link-belt-fed automatic) some of which had been made by Vickers while others were copies. They were already obsolescent at the outbreak of war owing to their comparatively slow rate of fire. The Japanese also utilized some captured Bofors 40 mm. cannon. Among the heavier anti-aircraft weapons were the 75–127 mm. range.

The type 88 was the standard Japanese anti-aircraft gun. It was a mobile weapon, being mounted on two rubber-tyred wheels, and was handled with skill and speed by Japanese gun-crews. This gun was 10 ft. long, weighed 5,400 lb., and had a maximum vertical range of 29,500 ft. (approximately the height of Mount Everest). Its practical rate of fire was 10·15 rounds a minute. The projectile had an average weight of 14 lb. and had a variety of fuses.

The type 3, a 76·2 mm. dual-purpose gun, was also widely used, although it was inferior to both the above weapons.

The type 99, 88 mm. anti-aircraft gun weighed 14,360 lb. but could be broken down into six separate parts for carrying purposes. It fired a 20 lb. projectile to a maximum vertical range of 31,000 ft.

The type 98, 100 mm. dual-purpose gun was a Navy weapon, originally designed for destroyers, but soon found to be extremely useful on land. It had a maximum vertical range of 44,000 ft., and a very high muzzle velocity (3,280 ft. per second). Its elevation was from −10 to +90 degrees. It fired a 28 lb. projectile. It was powered by electric motors and the projectile fuse was set automatically.

In contrast, the type 14, 105 mm. anti-aircraft gun was a failure. It jammed frequently and was too heavy for use on roads, for which purpose it had been constructed.

The type 10, 120 mm. dual-purpose anti-aircraft gun was the principal Japanese anti-aircraft gun in the later stages of the war. It was mounted on a conical steel pedestal, and this necessitated a concrete base or steel plate. Its vertical range was 33,000 ft.

The largest Japanese anti-aircraft gun was the type 89, a 127 mm. dual-purpose Navy gun. It was traversed and elevated electrically, and had automatic rammers and fuse-setters. It fired a 50 lb. projectile to 31,000 ft. at 12 rounds a minute per barrel.

The Japanese, having set out as a lightly mechanized army, gradually found themselves being defeated by greater firepower, by greater enemy mobility, and by their own tactical and strategic mistakes. They used the weapons described above with skill and courage but were eventually no match for the firepower of their opponents. It will be clear, however, from the above sample descriptions that the Japanese had the use of a wide variety of modern weapons, and were a modern army, well equipped for their self-appointed task.

RIFLES. Last in this survey of Japanese weapons, but by no means least, comes the rifle. Rifles, whether automatic or not, are the most personal weapons used in armies. Men may be crack shots with revolvers, skilled machine-gunners or members of courageous anti-tank crews, but none of these weapons is quite so much the 'soldier's friend' as his rifle. It is of course the first weapon he is issued with, and the first he fires; it introduces him to army life and becomes almost as much a part of him as his own limbs. He cleans it, cares for it, treats it perhaps with as much care as a pampered pet, and knows that when the enemy comes into view his rifle will either drop him at a distance or in the last resort provide a reasonable chance with the bayonet. The Japanese were ardent adherents of close-quarter fighting and would use a bayonet whenever the opportunity presented itself. Training for bayonet fighting was always a popular exercise, and it was obvious that a Japanese squad on bayonet drill, rushing and lunging at an imaginary adversary to the accompaniment of fierce guttural cries, had entered well into the spirit of the exercise. Bayonet design had remained virtually unchanged for years.

The standard issue rifles for the Japanese Army between 1941 and 1945 were 6·5 mm. and 7·7 mm. However, as with all armies, 'standard' issues often varied according to the year and place of manufacture. The basic model, the type 38, was notable for its long barrel and sliding bolt cover. Its overall length was 50·2 in., considerably longer than all other models except the type 97 sniper's rifle. The 38 weighed 8·95 lb. without the sling, had a maximum range of 4,300 yds. but an effective range of 450 yds.

A shorter version of the 38 was the type 38,

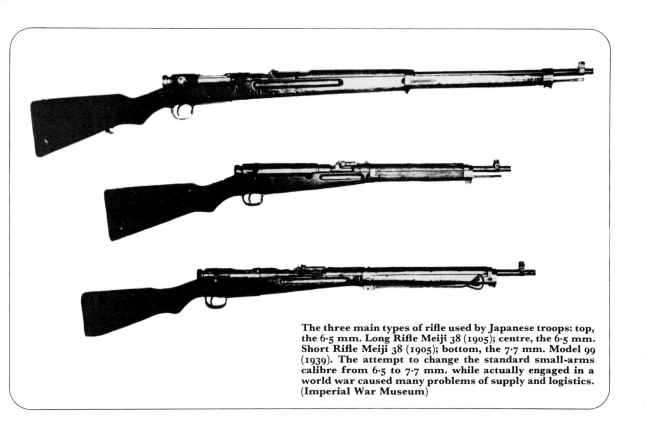

The three main types of rifle used by Japanese troops: top, the 6·5 mm. Long Rifle Meiji 38 (1905); centre, the 6·5 mm. Short Rifle Meiji 38 (1905); bottom, the 7·7 mm. Model 99 (1939). The attempt to change the standard small-arms calibre from 6·5 to 7·7 mm. while actually engaged in a world war caused many problems of supply and logistics. (Imperial War Museum)

6·5 mm. cavalry carbine. This was nearly two pounds lighter, but because of its 19 in. barrel it had a shorter range and a lesser muzzle velocity. Its total length was 38 in.

The type 38 (short) was longer than the carbine but not too long to become a problem for the soldier moving through difficult country such as thicket or jungle. Again, it was lighter than the basic 38, weighing 8·4 lb. without its sling. Its barrel length was 25·25 in., giving it a total length of 44·25 in.

A later model cavalry carbine was the type 44. This had a short barrel (19·37 in.) and an overall length of 38·25 in., but was considerably heavier than the other two short rifles, having a permanently attached short, spike bayonet. This bayonet folded when not required but could instantly be extended by pressing a plunger on the upper band of the rifle.

The sniper's rifle mentioned above had a long bolt handle, telescopic sights, and a monopod.

All these rifles had blade sights, and all fired semi-rimmed ammunition from 5-round clips. A round weighed 0·74 oz., of which 0·31 oz. was the weight of the bullet, and the remainder the weight of the charge.

During the war the 6·5 mm. rifles were gradually replaced by 7·7 mm. However, apart from the increase in calibre the basic characteristics remained much the same. The length was 44 in., of which 25·75 in. was taken up by the barrel. The maximum range and maximum effective range remained unchanged at 4,500 yds. and 450 yds. respectively. Ammunition was rimless and included ball, tracer and incendiary. The bullet was of course a little heavier, being 0·44 oz. The first models had useful refinements such as a folding monopod and anti-aircraft lead arms, but on the later models these were omitted, and the workmanship of the entire rifle was generally inferior.

FORTIFICATIONS

Although the concept of defensive warfare was anathema to Japanese thinking, the need to develop it was forced upon them. They called it 'retreat combat'. As will be seen later, they developed considerable expertise at it on the

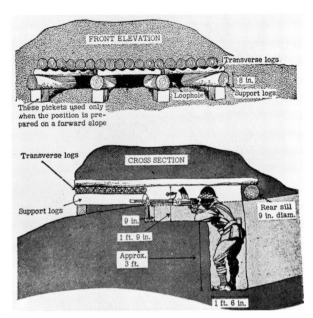

FRONT ELEVATION

Transverse logs

8 in.

Loophole

Support logs

These pickets used only when the position is prepared on a forward slope

Transverse logs

CROSS SECTION

Support logs

9 in.

1 ft. 9 in.

Approx. 3 ft.

Rear sill 9 in. diam.

1 ft. 6 in.

Front elevation and cross-section of Japanese light machine-gun pillbox

Pacific islands and in Burma. When, after the end of hostilities, the Allies decided to carry out the planned Malaya landings 'for practice', they were impressed by what they found in the way of defences, and were relieved to think they had not had to carry out these landings against manned positions.

Nevertheless, it should not be thought that the Japanese ever lacked knowledge or experience of how to make fortifications; they had developed fortifications as part of their offensive skills in a wide variety of territories. Initially, Japanese fire-power had been concentrated on the perimeter but subsequently the Army showed considerable skill at defence in depth. The offensive aspect of defence in depth was preserved by the use of underground passages from which Japanese soldiers would emerge when the ground had been overrun. Somewhat disconcertingly for their opponents, the exits were so well camouflaged and concealed that they were not easily detected. Japanese skill lay not so much in their use of nets and paint as in the use they made of materials. In some areas the exits would be covered with vegetation transplanted with such skill that it was still growing; in more barren areas the rocks and stones would have been so arranged that the eye would be led away from the vital area and so fail to detect it. Dummy defences, often amazingly realistic even at close

quarters, were used to shepherd attackers into positions well prepared to receive them.

FOXHOLES. The foxhole was the simplest form of defensive position and the Japanese were adept at constructing them in unlikely, and thus unsuspected, places. More permanent sites were often lined with concrete, but much the same degree of protection was obtained by the use of earth and logs. Coconut-palm logs were widely used, and proved to be splinterproof for some time against bombs and shells. They were normally effective defence against anything but a direct hit. This combination of earth and timber has been used in defences all over the world since prehistoric times but in World War II it came as a surprise to find that it could absorb much of the shock of high explosive.

PILLBOXES. The Japanese made extensive use of pillboxes in all theatres of war. They housed single soldiers or small groups, and were sited very close together. At Tasawa they were placed all round the island, about 25 yards apart, 50 yards above high-water line. On Iwo Jima 900 pillboxes were sited in 1,000 sq. yds. Obviously all pillboxes varied considerably in size and defence value. The small ones usually measured $6 \times 6 \times 6$ ft., but there were larger ones of all sizes. When available, $\frac{1}{2}$ in. steel reinforcing rods were used.

Apart from the direct hit, there were two main hazards to the pillboxes. One was that debris would obscure the embrasure and thus make it useless; this was countered by digging a ditch for debris to fall into. The second was the grenade which would be rolled in. As a counter to the grenade, which had a four-second fuse and thus could not be thrown out in time, a well was made into which it could be kicked. Although it would explode lethally and unpleasantly, its worst effects would be blunted.

CAVES. No other nation has ever made such full use of caves as the Japanese, possibly because no one needed to, but it is undeniable that Japanese cave defence gave enormous trouble to their attackers. Flame-throwers and grenades would clear the outer chambers but leave the interiors untouched. Furthermore, the caves incorporated

1 Ittōhei (Private 1st Class),
1st Imperial Guard Infantry, late 1930s
2 Shō-i (2nd Lieutenant) of engineers,
service dress, late 1930s
3 Chū-i (1st Lieutenant) of infantry,
China, late 1930s

MICHAEL YOUENS

A

1 Chūsa (Lieutenant-Colonel),
  winter dress, late 1930s
2 Infantryman, winter field dress,
  late 1930s
3 Gochō (Corporal),
  transitional uniform. 1938

B

1 Shōsa (Major) of cavalry,
  1938 service dress
2 Nitōhei (Private, 2nd Class)
  of infantry, 1941
3 Gochō (Corporal),
  machine-gun team, 1941

MICHAEL YOUENS

C

1 Jōtōhei (Senior Private),
winter fatigue dress, 1941
2 Heichō (Lance-Corporal),
trópical field dress, 1942
3 Shōsa (Major) of artillery,
tropical service dress, 1942

D

MICHAEL YOUENS

1 Shōshō (Major-General),
  1938-pattern officer's coat
2 Infantryman,
  tropical field dress, 1941
3 Jūn-i (Warrant Officer)
  of armoured troops, 1942

MICHAEL YOUENS

E

1 Chū-i (1st Lieutenant),
  Army Air Force
2 Infantryman,
  sniper's cape, 1940
3 Infantryman,
  tropical fatigue dress, 1940

F

1 Trainee parachutist, 1943
2 Nitōhei (Private, 2nd Class) in early sun helmet
3 Gunsō (Sergeant) of parachute troops, tropical service dress, 1943

MICHAEL YOUENS

G

1 Officer, tropical field service dress, 1944-5
2 Tropical field dress, 1944-5
3 Heichō (Lance-Corporal),
  parachute troops, 1944

H

MICHAEL YOUENS

many mutually supporting positions in their depth. Petrol bombs eventually proved the most effective anti-cave defence weapon. On Iwo Jima, however, the caves had been so modified, and so reinforced with concrete, that the Japanese were able to make them into near-impregnable gun emplacements. One of the most disconcerting aspects of cave positions was the ease with which the defender maintained intercommunication.

Apart from this deep dugout type of fortification the Japanese developed considerable expertise in surface field fortification. When the opposition was light, as in China, these looked like small medieval castles, and like them they abounded in underground passages to the adjoining strongpoints. They were usually of stone or concrete. Although easily breached by bomb or shell, they were effective enough against the small-arms fire which was all they normally encountered. They had a variety of uses, serving as storage depots, observa-

Japanese mountain blockhouse in China. Note subterranean tunnel pattern

tion stations or administration headquarters. Surface fortifications were sometimes necessary when the ground could not be dug, either because it was of rock or because it was waterlogged. But when the surface could be worked the Japanese soldier dug in with considerable speed and efficiency, and would readily construct a veritable labyrinth of underground passages even though he did not expect to stay long in the area.

Plan of Japanese cave position in Luzon, Philippine Islands

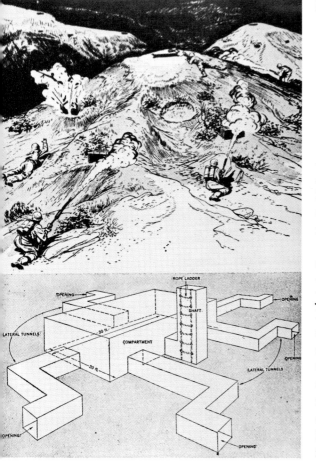

The Far East Theatre

At the outbreak of the war in the East the Japanese Army had fifty-one operational divisions, each including approximately 18,000 men. Not all these could be used in offensive operations. Some were needed to hold ground already won in China and Manchuria; nor would it be safe to denude Korea and Japan entirely. Fortunately for the Japanese their prospective opponents, in the area which the Japanese proposed to convert into the 'Greater East Asia Co-Prosperity Sphere', were very thin on the ground. Furthermore, when a nation decides to go to war and invade other countries the troops used in spearhead thrusts invariably tend to be better armed, equipped and motivated than those likely to oppose them. This was especially true in the vast area known as the Far Eastern Theatre. Burma, which looks an insignificant strip of territory on the map, is more than five times as large as England, and many of the areas where fighting took place were separated from one another by hundreds of miles of sea or barren terrain.

THE PACIFIC ISLANDS

It is not easy to realize that a few insignificant dots seen on the map are important strategic points in a vast complex of islands. The Philippine Islands cover 115,000 square miles and are over 7,000 in number, some of them large enough to be easily picked out. When it comes to the Carolines, the Marianas, and the Okinawa (= 'long rope') groups it is impossible to conceive of these as vital fronts on one of the bitterest wars ever fought. Who today knows that the Admiralties, for instance, are a group of islands north-east of New Guinea, or that in February 1944 these were an area of critical strategic importance? But they had a good harbour, known as Seeadler, and their capture would pierce the Japanese defensive circle in the south-west Pacific. Yet the Admiralties, which the Dutch had first discovered in 1616 and which had never been properly mapped, had rain-forests, jungle, coral reefs, mountains, mangrove swamps, a hot sultry climate, and 4,300 dedicated Japanese defenders. Two and a half months later the Americans counted 3,280 Japanese dead and 75 captured; the remainder had presumably been buried by the Japanese themselves. For the Americans at that time it was an extremely venturesome operation, and could well have ended in failure; instead, it was an enormous and vital success. But who today has heard of it, or even of the name of the place where the battles were fought?

Among the interesting features of that battle was the repair of a Japanese 120 mm. gun, made in 1914. The Japanese gunners had removed the telescopic sights but the American gunners succeeded in using it to plant forty rounds into the Japanese force on the near-by Pityilu Island.

The Japanese had certainly taken on a considerable task when they set out on their path of expansion. Their aim, of course, was to secure vital supplies of oil and raw material. In consequence they soon found themselves fighting over an area stretching the length of the distance between Canada and Berlin and extending as far south as Cairo.

PEARL HARBOR. Initially they had enormous success. On 7 December 1941, 350 carrier-based aircraft had struck without warning at Pearl Harbor, the base of the United States Pacific Fleet in the Hawaiian Islands. Within less than thirty minutes they had sunk three battleships, capsized one, damaged four more, three cruisers, and three destroyers, destroyed 188 aircraft and inflicted nearly 4,000 casualties. Their aim was to cripple the American war effort in the Pacific beyond hope of recovery. But, devastating as this blow was, it failed of its full effect; the American carriers, on which so much would later depend, were at sea. Furthermore this unexpected, unannounced attack stimulated the Americans to a degree of effort at which even they themselves were surprised. But their revenge was still far off – in time as well as place.

Within days of their attack on Pearl Harbor the Japanese were in Guam, Wake Island and the Philippine Islands, though some of these held out till 10 May 1942.

MALAYA

Meanwhile the Japanese were equally active elsewhere. On the night of 7 December they appeared unannounced off the coast of Malaya, and proceeded to inflict a series of disasters on British, Indian, and Australian troops there. They first destroyed the few obsolete planes on the airfields, and then achieved one of the most spectacular successes of the war by sinking the new battleship *Prince of Wales* and the slightly older battle-cruiser *Repulse* by aircraft. From then onwards they were able to bomb with impunity, often using high-altitude pattern-bombing with groups of 60 Navy Zeros at a time, and to land at will along the peninsula. They also introduced tanks in what was believed to be terrain entirely unsuitable for mechanized vehicles, and refused to regard the jungle as the obstacle it was thought to be. Greatly aided by inept command on the part of the enemy, they were able to capture large quantities of war material. Finally they laid siege to Singapore itself. Singapore, an island about the size of the Isle of

Wight, had been described as a 'fortress of steel ringed by mighty guns'. It was in fact a lightly defended sub-tropical island with a population of over a million Asians. A few days before it surrendered – with water-supplies cut off, and a rapidly mounting toll of casualties among non-combatants – a new British division, 22,000 strong, but without most of its arms, which had been sunk on the way in, landed with no hope of restoring the situation, and at once became prisoners. With them in captivity were the smaller number of men who had fought their way down the peninsula, falling back from one position to another on instructions that were as demoralizing as they were incomprehensible. But, here and there, the defeated British had earned the respect of their conquerors, before the latter pressed on to Java, Sumatra and the other islands of the Dutch East Indies group, as it was then called. Finally, the shouts of 'Banzai!' ('Victory!') were heard in New Guinea, and the Japanese Army was drawing near to Australia.

HONG KONG AND BORNEO

Hong Kong was even more vulnerable than Malaya. Britain had believed that Malaya could be defended if adequate air and naval power were available and were sent in time; of Hong Kong it was believed that its garrison of six battalions would at least succeed in drawing off a considerable Japanese effort from more dangerous employment elsewhere. Hong Kong comprised the Island itself and a small mainland peninsula opposite known as Kowloon. The Island drew half its water from mainland sources and all its water-supply was vulnerable. The garrison had no real chance from the start, although this would not have been guessed from its fighting spirit. Eventually, numbers and airpower told, and the last outpost had to lay down its arms on 25 December 1941.

Borneo was not attacked until 16 December, with the main thrust going in on the 24th. The aim of the British defence was to destroy as much strategic material as possible before leaving. The fighting was over within a few days, but was fierce and bitter while it lasted. There was, of course, no hope of defending these out-stations against power-ful naval and air forces, and the best that could be done was to inflict as much damage and delay as possible.

BURMA

The Japanese Army did not invade Burma till January 1942 but then displayed the same speed, flexibility and offensive spirit as had paid handsome dividends elsewhere. The best way to visualize Burma is to point the right hand downwards, and imagine the forefinger extending itself along western Thailand towards Malaya. The gaps between the fingers give a fair idea of the position of the river valleys: the Chindwin, the Irrawaddy and the Salween. As the Japanese Army poured into Burma their higher command believed that the vital step to the domination of the Far East had now been taken. China would be cut off from Allied support, the Western Allies would be pushed back in the west as far as they had been in the east, and the invasion of India could be mounted at leisure. This was partly but not wholly true. Burma, with its rice, wolfram and oil, was a superb and much needed base. Strategically it had many advantages. There was a good road and rail network and the area of Japanese Army occupation was the driest and least malarial part of the country. The rains of the monsoon can nullify all the efforts of an army. The wettest parts of Britain have less than 30 in. of rain a year; much of Burma has 200 in., some parts as much as 500 in. The effect can be easily imagined. Dry, dusty roads and tracks suddenly become quagmires of liquid mud. Under these conditions the Japanese Army made extensive use of 'hand-wagons', small carts which would normally take a load of about 6 cwt. As the Japanese strained to get these wagons along muddy tracks it was not unusual to see a soldier fall face downwards in the mud and almost suffocate before someone pulled him up with more annoyance than kindness. Rivers would be transformed overnight; what today was a slow fordable stream might tomorrow be a raging torrent, twenty feet higher, swirling down a mass of vegetation, tree trunks and other dangerous debris. The Japanese Army built bridges over many areas – with prisoner-of-war labour. Piles were driven into the river-bed in a process that required no

Note helmet tapes, machine-gun spares cases slung round the crew's shoulders and officer's field uniform. (Imperial War Museum)

machinery whatever. Over each pile a derrick was erected, and the driving force was supplied by a weight raised by ropes and then dropped like a hammer. The "coolies" pulling the ropes would spend a good part of the time standing in the shallower parts of the river. These wooden bridges proved amazingly resilient to the force of the monsoon-swollen rivers but, if a large enough pile of debris built up, they were liable to be swept away.

History records the severe suffering of armies from malarial infection. It is said that the decline of the Roman Empire was due to the effect on the inhabitants of Rome of malaria from near-by marshes, and in more recent times whole countries have been incapacitated by its enfeebling effects. The disease, carried by the anopheles mosquito, takes several forms, some of which, such as cerebral malaria, can kill rapidly. But for the most part malaria causes a gradual debilitation which affects the spleen, makes the patient weak and anaemic, and often paves the way for other more lethal illnesses such as blackwater fever; and no man fights efficiently with a temperature of 104 degrees or over. The cause of malaria was unknown until the 1890s, when an English doctor, Ronald Ross, eventually linked it with the anopheles mosquito and devised a cure. Quinine, which is made from the bark of a tree, not only cures malaria but can also be used as a prophylactic. The Japanese Army, in addition to having some of the healthier parts of Burma as its base, had recently captured Java, the source of the world's main quinine supply. Thus they were in

a vastly better position than the British and Indian troops opposing them, although the latter were soon employing synthetic cures for malaria such as mepacrine. (Owing, possibly, to ingenious propaganda many Allied soldiers believed that regular doses of mepacrine induced impotence; it was therefore sometimes necessary to ensure that men took their due prophylactic. No such legend was attached to quinine, and the Japanese were pleased to take as much as they needed.)

In addition to the resources of Burma the Japanese Army now had control of Malaya, the source of half the world supply of tin, and one-third of the world's natural rubber; they had the oil resources of Java, and huge supplies of captured British, Dutch and American war materials. On the other hand many of the oil wells had been blown up, many factories had been burnt, and the utilizing of these new resources presented very considerable problems.

The war in Burma was often bitterly, but not inaccurately, called the 'forgotten war'. To the soldiers of both sides it could well seem so. The war in the desert and in other theatres was comparatively simple and clear-cut; but the geography and topography of Burma were so confusing that it was felt, not unnaturally, that no one could really understand what was going on. The Japanese, of course, had not this feeling so strongly as the Allies, but it was not unknown even to them. This was not China, Malaya or the Philippines; this was a green hell where nature was no less hostile than man.

The Japanese Supreme Commander for the southern region was Field-Marshal Count Juichi Terauchi. He was a man of enormous power, and corresponding ability. Formerly he had been Minister of War and a member of the Supreme War Council, which advised the Emperor in his conduct of the war. (Whether or not the Emperor really used the power he possessed is still a matter of debate, but it seems unlikely.) Supreme War Council decisions were conveyed to Imperial General Headquarters in Tokyo. I.G.H. was a combined Army/Navy establishment which included the Chiefs of Staff from both arms. (The Army commanded most of the Japanese Air Force although a small portion came under Navy command). When therefore Terauchi received his orders from I.G.H. they were likely to be the orders he wished to receive. However, the very success of the early Japanese military thrusts now tended to make commanders at all levels require more of their men than, in that climate and against that opposition, they were capable of delivering. This became increasingly true when hostilities settled down to a war of attrition. Moreover, as often happens, a high degree of expertise in one aspect of war can lead to disaster when the enemy introduce a new and more sophisticated technique. In Burma this was air supply. In their first successes the Japanese divisions had owed much to the outflanking techniques already described. British units, therefore, who found themselves cut off, had to force a way through to their supply base or perish for lack of ammunition or food. Any action they took to reopen the supply line inevitably weakened the position further forward, and the result was often a Japanese victory. This situation changed entirely when air drops were fully in operation, for not only was the forward unit well supplied but the Japanese 'hooks' and 'pincers' were now themselves highly vulnerable. A further development occurred when certain Allied units, noting that the Japanese line of communication was long and thinly stretched, cut it with a parachute drop, and created administrative chaos. The Japanese response to the vulnerability of their line of communication was to show the utmost skill in camouflage and concealment. This concealment was not only effective from the air but also highly skilled at ground-level. Throughout the war the Allies could never be quite sure whether they were on clear ground or whether they were advancing into a strongly fortified 'bunker' position which would suddenly come alive in a blaze of cross-fire and be held with the utmost tenacity, offering no safety for two or three weeks because of snipers lying up in cunningly hidden positions. One Japanese soldier captured by the 16th Punjabis in 1944 – it was a very rare event to capture a Japanese soldier alive at that stage of the war – was wounded, hopelessly cut off, and had not eaten or drunk for three days. Nevertheless he made an attempt to use a grenade against Allied motor transport – and it very nearly succeeded.

The first real check to the Japanese Army in Burma came in the Arakan. The Arakan is a narrow strip of land consisting of steep hills, swamp and *padi* fields (*padi* = 'growing rice'). Akyab is its port. In January 1943 the British/Indian Army had made a vigorous attempt to reconquer the Arakan, but the Japanese had been well dug-in; although the offensive spirit of the Allies had taken them deep into strong Japanese positions, they were held and then counter-attacked. The leading spirit in the counter-attack was Colonel Tanahashi. Both sides, in this forgotten early stage, showed courage and skill of the highest order. Finally at a cost of 2,500 battle casualties the attempted Allied comeback ground to a halt with no gain at all. The Japanese felt renewed confidence; the Allies, although now aware that the Japanese soldier for all his toughness was not invincible, looked at the future with subdued optimism. Air supply might well be the answer to the Japanese but for the moment it was not easy to visualize, for the Japanese Navy Zeros were faster and more manoeuvrable than the British Hurricanes.

Air power was of course vital, and fortunately for the Allies it was increased. It was essential for keeping China still in the war; that is to say, well supplied, and this involved flying over 'the Hump', a treacherous mountain range, into China. The saga of the flights over 'the Hump' have no place here, but merit a book to themselves. But even the spectacularly brave and enterprising efforts of the Chindits, who, commanded by General Orde Wingate, made deep penetrations into Japanese-held territory, had little effect on the Japanese war effort.

Both sides in Burma, and in all tropical areas, were subjected to a variety of tormenting and distracting diseases. Apart from malaria and its sequelae there were typhus, typhoid, cholera, ulcers, dengue, sand-fly fever, diarrhoea, and a wide variety of skin infections. Of these cholera was the swiftest and most feared. It was transmitted by water and seemed to break out soon after the onset of the monsoon. It could be contracted orally or through a graze in the skin. Another less prevalent though equally lethal illness was leptospirosis ('Japanese river fever'), which lurks in inviting jungle pools. It is carried by infected rats and at that stage was incurable. Dysentery and diarrhoea were all too easily contracted, and a semi-chronic form of the latter was widespread. Skin infections varied from maddening but harmless prickly-heat rash to scabies and jungle ulcers. Scabies is easily eliminated if the right medicines are available but jungle ulcers were more formidable. A scratch from a bamboo thorn – some bamboo thorn was like barbed wire – could result in a growing ulcer that would spread and eat its way down to the bone. For a man on an isolated patrol this could mean inability to march; and if you could not move in the jungle your chance of survival was slight.

In Burma, as elsewhere in the Pacific, some Japanese soldiers persevered in fighting with bandages tied above their wounds at the pressure points. This would enable them to fight a little longer, though making gangrene inevitable; such was their standard of dedication and tenacity.

KOHIMA AND IMPHAL

The great Japanese offensive to invade India was launched on 15 March 1944. The Japanese aimed at the Brahmaputra Valley, where they could overrun the airfields which were supplying China. Following that, they planned to push on into India. The ensuing battle, which lasted three months, centred mainly on Kohima in the north and Imphal in the south. For both sides it was an epic occasion. Unfortunately this theatre of war has never received the attention from writers which it deserves, but it should be noted that the attack, launched with every fraction of impetus the Japanese could put into it, was met with equal stubbornness.

One of the most remarkable Japanese actions at this time was their performance in hauling their guns up a 1,000 ft. cliff and reaching a vital position in the British lines from which they were only eliminated by being killed to a man. The respect which the Japanese earned for their courage in this area, however, was completely wiped out by the behaviour of about seventy Japanese, including six officers, who cold-bloodedly massacred the patients and staff of the field hospital at M.D.S. (Main Dressing Station) Hill. A similar massacre had taken place at the Alexandra Hospital, Singapore, in February 1942. Both occasions were appalling, senseless, and not really in keeping with the Bushido attitudes. The

only explanation is that those who committed these atrocities were so imbued with fanaticism that they thought they were performing a useful military service in killing men who might fight again and those instrumental in saving the lives of the wounded.

Militarily the Japanese Army showed infinite courage and resource. In their night attacks they managed to assume a non-human appearance by using huge and hideous masks. The upper part of the mask was designed to draw Allied fire to a point where it could do no harm. But, with all its effort, the Japanese offensive failed.

ON THE DEFENSIVE

As the tide of war turned, and the Japanese fell back, their skill in other than offensive activity began to show itself. In Burma, as in the Pacific islands, the Japanese Army adapted itself to a defensive strategy, however contrary to their philosophy of war, and did so with commendable thoroughness. Their defensive tunnelling, some of which is illustrated in the accompanying sketches and photographs, displayed great skill, and their defence was maintained literally to the last man. In the unsuccessful Arakan offensive the Japanese lost 53,000 men and 250 guns. But the 14th Army opposing them had also sustained heavy losses, though not of material. In this battle, the opposing sides in one sector had been separated for two weeks by no more than the width of a tennis court.

Eventually, when the Japanese decided to withdraw to Toungoo after many months of hard fighting, it was too late. They were ambushed and cut off; on 3 May 1945 General Slim's army retook Rangoon.

In Burma the Japanese Army had been beaten in a long and dogged campaign. In the Pacific islands Japanese soldiers hung on to the last with the same grim tenacity. The fighting at Iwo Jima and Okinawa was typical of the resolution with which they would have defended their homeland, had they been required to do so.

IWO JIMA. This is a small volcanic island $5\frac{1}{2}$ miles long by $2\frac{1}{2}$ miles wide (the volcano is extinct). It lies half-way between the Marianas and Tokyo, and was therefore of great value as a forward air

Japanese prisoner in Singapore, 1945. (Imperial War Museum)

base for the Americans. It was pounded with over 6,000 tons of bombs and 22,000 shells before the assault went in with 30,000 Marines. The Japanese garrison, numbering 20,000, had fortified the position with the utmost ingenuity and here, as elsewhere, made the maximum use of mortars; the Marines suffered 10,000 casualties. Eventually when Iwo Jima fell in February 1945, of the Japanese 20,000 only 216 were alive to be taken prisoner.

OKINAWA. This island was larger, being 67 miles long by 20 miles wide, and was defended by 90,000 Japanese under General Mitsuru Ushijima. The pattern of the fighting differed somewhat from that on Iwo Jima. The landings, after heavy initial bombardments, were deceptively easy; the Japanese were reserving themselves for a bigger occasion later. The heavy fighting did not begin till a week after the first attack, which had taken place on 1 April 1945. At Okinawa an attempt was made by the Japanese Navy to relieve their hard-pressed garrison, only to result in the loss of all but one of their capital ships. They were still able, however, to turn the full force of their kamikazes on to the American fleet; some 3,000 were used and the effect was dramatic. But this was, in the last resort, a war of metal, explosions and attrition. By the end of April the Americans had 160,000 men on Okinawa, grim though their position was. Gradually they gained the upper hand, and on 21 June 1945 General Ushijima and his Chief of Staff Lieutenant-General Cho both ceremonially committed *hara-kiri* at dawn. They and their garrison had done all and more than could have been expected. The Americans had incurred 49,000 casualties as well as huge losses of ships and material.

RAIDS ON JAPAN. The war was already lost by the Japanese but that did not, of course, mean that it was anywhere near to being over. There were still plenty of Japanese soldiers to fight, mainly on the Chinese mainland, and there was the entire population of Japan already hard in training to die for their country. But the real damage had already been done by the devastating bombing which had been continuous since the previous March. The first B-29 bombers had appeared over Tokyo in November 1944 and gradually the aerial onslaught had been built up until, on 10 March 1945, 190,000 incendiary bombs had burnt out 42 per cent of the whole of Tokyo; 89,000 people were killed, 41,000 were injured, and 276,000 homes were destroyed. And it was not on Tokyo alone that these devastating fire raids took place. In the same month Nagoya, Osaka and Kobe suffered raids which inflicted thousands of casualties. Other raids took place in April and May, by which time a host of smaller targets were also being attacked. Sixty-five of the larger cities were bombed and burnt. Japanese industry was very widely dispersed, and there were places in the hills of Japan which never saw a bomb, but these great raids on major industrial cities dislocated the country's production as a whole, caused hunger and disease and brought the population within sight of famine. Nevertheless both Japanese and Americans knew that Japan is a highly developed industrial country, with a population verging on 90 million. Even a million or more casualties would not

The end. Japanese soldiers bow in the direction of Hirohito's palace after the announcement of Japan's surrender in August 1945. (Keystone)

greatly affect the Japanese war effort; the Japanese would fight for their homeland with a tenacity and fanaticism surpassing the record of any other war theatre. There were still millions of soldiers under arms, thousands of planes and thousands of suicide pilots. Oil and other resources were scarce, but they would last long enough to inflict fearful devastation on any invader. In August 1945 the Japanese Army had 55 divisions to employ for home defence, a total of just over $2\frac{1}{4}$ million men. Behind them were another million supporters who would fight, too, if their turn came.

FINAL SURRENDER

But on 6 August 1945 a single atomic bomb was dropped on Hiroshima, causing nearly 100,000 casualties. Hiroshima was an army H.Q. with arsenals and over 100,000 soldiers. On 8 August Russia declared war on Japan, and the Red Army invaded Manchuria. On the following day a second atomic bomb was dropped, this time on Nagasaki, causing another 80,000 casualties. There was no point in Japan trying to continue the war, but if she did, the final Allied assault could well cost them at least a million casualties. Fortunately for all, and especially for the Allied prisoners of war in Japanese hands, the Emperor, after consultation with his Cabinet, agreed to surrender. Japan ceased to fight and on 15 August 1945 one of the costliest wars in history came to an end. Had it not ceased at the time and in the way that it did, Japan would perhaps be remembered for other reasons than its being the first (and we hope the last) country to receive an atomic bomb. For Japan is mostly hills and mountains, and if the Japanese had decided to continue to the bitter end, not only in Japan but in Thailand, Malaya, Manchuria and China, that end would have been very bitter indeed.

32

The Plates

A1 Ittōhei (Private 1st Class), 1st Imperial Guard Infantry, late 1930s

The khaki service cap was the normal headgear for all ranks in the mid-1930s; it is piped around the crown seam in red, and has a red band, irrespective of branch of service. The peak is black leather, as is the chinstrap. The normal yellow metal star cap badge is replaced in Imperial Guard units by a star supported by a small spray of foliage. The 1930-pattern tunic is worn, in a rather heavy woollen cloth of a mustard khaki shade. On the stand-up collar appear swallow-tail tabs in the branch of service colour – here, the scarlet of the infantry – bearing the regimental number in the form of a yellow metal '1'. All buttons are yellow metal. The insignia of rank appear on the shoulders, in the form of strips of cloth fastened transversely to small loops; in this case they bear the two yellow stars of an Ittōhei. The background of these tabs is plain red. A waist-belt and shoulder-braces of brown hide support three ammunition pouches – the third is worn centrally at the rear – and a bayonet frog behind the left hip. The front pouches each hold six 5-round clips, the rear pouch twelve clips. The trousers are secured by fabric puttees, and the boots are brown leather, front-laced, ankle-length items with hobnails. The rifle is the Arisaka 6·5 mm. Model 38 of 1905.

A2 Shō-i (2nd Lieutenant) of engineers, service dress, late 1930s

This officer, in parade order, wears a rather tauter and smarter version of the service cap, with plain gold star cap badge. His 1930-pattern tunic is worn without a waist-belt, the suspender for his sword-scabbard passing under the tunic to a concealed fastening. The collar tabs bear the regimental number on the burgundy-red background of the engineers, and his rank tabs are worn on the shoulder in the usual way – in this case, two red transverse stripes and a gold star on a gold ground. The white gloves are worn with parade order, and the trousers have no turn-ups. The plain military sword with leather-covered scabbard is decorated with a blue silk tassel, indicating a company-grade officer.

A3 Chū-i (1st Lieutenant) of infantry, China, late 1930s

The service cap gave way to the conical field cap for wear on campaign; officers' and other ranks' field caps were identical in design, differing only in quality. This subaltern wears the 1930-pattern tunic and trousers, with infantry distinctions and rank tabs in the conventional manner. Although puttees or buckled leather leggings, both worn with ankle-length lace-up boots, would be more in keeping with the infantry branch, this officer

Japanese staff officer, member of the party which represented the Emperor at the 1937 Coronation of H.M. George VI. He wears the 1930-pattern service dress; note that as he is away from his unit, the collar patches in branch of service colours bear no regimental numbers. (Keystone)

33

Japanese infantry in China. They wear the old-pattern sleeveless fleece-lined coat, and carry their equipment in 'hold-all' rolls slung around the body. (Imperial War Museum)

prefers privately purchased riding boots – like many of his contemporaries. It should be pointed out that all officers' uniforms were privately purchased, thus accounting for the variations sometimes observed in shade, cut and detail. This 1st Lieutenant wears a field service waist-belt of quilted fabric, and is trying out the wooden holster/ shoulder stock attachment for his 8 mm. Nambu automatic pistol. (For many years the existence of the stocked Nambu was disputed, but an example is currently preserved in the Imperial War Museum, London.) An extra star on the shoulder tabs distinguishes his rank from that of the previous figure.

B1 Chūsa (Lieutenant-Colonel), winter dress (Manchuria), late 1930s
In the severe winter conditions faced by the Japanese in China and Manchuria various cold-weather gear was issued. The woollen cap is lined with fur or fleece, and has fur ear-flaps which are

tied on top of the head when not required. The heavy sailcloth coat is thickly lined with fur or fleece, and has a fur collar and cuffs. Because of the difficulty of moving with agility in these garments there is provision for the sleeves to be unbuttoned and removed when not required. Just above the join of the sleeve a rank patch is worn. The boots are of felt, with high-welded rubber soles and pile lining. The pile-lined felt mittens have an 'extra' woollen trigger finger below the index finger, for obvious reasons. The field-glass case is of glazed hide.

B2 Infantryman, winter field dress, late 1930s
The old-style helmet worn by this soldier, with its pronounced 'peak', was being progressively replaced during the late 1930s. It is held in place by tapes from above and behind the ears which are tied beneath the chin. It is worn here over a woollen toque, issued in cold weather. The sleeves of the 1930 tunic are exposed by the early-pattern sleeveless sheepskin coat worn by other ranks in

the field. The ankle-length pile-lined felt boots are protected by thick felt leggings, also pile-lined and buckling up the outside of the leg. The Meiji 38 rifle is carried. Field equipment includes a hide pack, with the hair left on, round which a blanket is strapped in horseshoe shape; a waterproof shelter-half is rolled and strapped to the top, and the nest of kidney-shaped aluminium mess-tins is strapped to the back. An entrenching spade, with detachable handle, is carried in a cotton cover on the left of the pack; these were issued on the ratio of two shovels to one pick. A water canteen of painted aluminium rests on the right hip in a strap cradle, with a sling passing over the left shoulder. A heavy cotton duck haversack is worn on the left hip, again slung on a crossbelt, and the bayonet hangs from the waist-belt underneath this.

B3 Gochō (Corporal), transitional uniform, 1938
The strangely shaped 'turtle-armour' being studied with some concern by this N.C.O. was used in the Sino-Japanese War to enable men to crawl in safety over ground swept by enemy small-arms fire; it also acted as a sort of mobile pillbox for snipers. The Corporal wears the 1930 uniform but with the insignia conventions of the newly issued 1938 uniform; the rank patches have been moved from the shoulder to the collar, and the swallow-tail collar tabs with regimental and branch distinctions have been discarded. The patch on the right arm – a single yellow bar on a red rectangle – was worn by corporals, sergeants and sergeant-majors alike, indicating a class of N.C.O. rather than a rank.

C1 Shōsa (Major) of cavalry, 1938 service dress
The field cap had now replaced the service cap for all practical purposes, being worn even on parade. The new tunic was of a greener shade of khaki than the 1930 model, and had a turn-down collar. This Captain, as a cavalry officer, wears pegged riding breeches and spurred boots; officers of other branches sometimes wore the same outfit in preference to puttees, leather leggings and the semi-breeches or 'pantaloons' normally worn. The insignia of rank are worn on the collar, and the M-shaped badge above the right breast pocket is in the branch colour – in this case, cavalry green. These badges were seldom observed after 1940.

The leather waist-belt was often replaced by a heavily stitched fabric belt in the field. A shoulder-strap supports the holster for the 1925 Model 14 automatic pistol, an unimpressive weapon of 8 mm. calibre. Haversack, canteen and gas-mask case are also slung on shoulder-straps. The fine-quality sword – perhaps a family heirloom centuries old, newly mounted in the regulation army fittings – is decorated with the red cord and tassel of a field-grade officer.

C2 Nitōhei (Private 2nd Class) of infantry, 1941
The old helmet has been replaced by the new pot-shaped model with embossed star insignia. The 1938 field uniform is worn, with full equipment. The rank badges – a single yellow star on a red ground – are worn on the collar. The pack, with blanket and raincoat or shelter-half rolled and strapped to it, is worn on the back, and the handle of the spade can be seen above the shoulder. Two haversacks are worn, for personal effects, rations, grenades or any of the many pieces of equipment required in the field. The canteen is worn on the right hip on a leather strap. The puttees are cross-gartered with tapes, to prevent

A party of Japanese officials, visiting manœuvres at Shimoshiza during the 1930s, are shown a soldier wearing a gas-mask and a camouflage netting cape. Note the method of wearing the sword and map-case by the officer on the right. (Radio Times Hulton)

35

This group of infantry wear the 1938 tunic and later-pattern circular steel helmet. The officer carries his scabbarded sword rather than wearing it slung – a characteristic of the traditional use of Japanese swords. Note the thirty-round Hotchkiss-type strip feed of the Model 92 machine-gun. (Imperial War Museum)

D2 Heichō (Lance-Corporal), *tropical field dress*
This soldier wears a thin drill version of the 1938 uniform, of greenish-khaki cotton. His helmet is covered with hessian, netting and applied foliage. The insignia of his rank are worn on collar and arm; they were often omitted in the field. In place of leather boots he wears the light, comfortable, silent *tabi* – a split or 'camel-toed' boot of canvas and rubber with a heavily cleated sole. He wears his kit in a fabric hold-all slung round his body and tied with a sash – this is simply a piece of canvas with tying-cords, into which necessities for

their coming loose at an awkward moment. The trousers of the 1938 uniform are full semi-breeches, and the tight puttees give them almost the appearance of knickerbockers. The rifle is the Meiji 38.

C3 Gochō (Corporal), *machine-gun team, 1941*
In the field there was a good deal of latitude in the arrangement of kit, especially among troops with specialist equipment to carry. The glazed leather carrying-case for the spare parts and tools of the Model 92 7·7 mm. Hotchkiss-type machine-gun is carried on a shoulder-strap by this N.C.O. The rank insignia are conventional. A netting cover is fitted to the helmet for the attachment of foliage.

D1 Jōtōhei (Senior Private), *winter fatigue dress*
Carrying his shovel in the characteristic manner, this junior N.C.O. is dressed as he might be for, say, snow-clearing on an airfield in China or the Aleutians. The woollen toque can be pulled tight around the face by a draw-string, and extends down into the collar. The normal 1938 field uniform is worn under the heavily padded canvas overalls. The three stars of the *Jōtōhei* appear on red tabs on the collar, and the thick red chevron of this rank is worn on the upper arm. (Narrow red chevrons, 'diligence stripes' for meritorious conduct, were also worn on the arm in this position.) The shoes are of felt, fur-lined and high-welted for protection against damp.

Japanese soldier with one-man float for crossing water obstacles; he carries hand-paddles and wears a kapok-filled life-jacket. (Keystone)

Hirohito visits army manœuvres in 1930-pattern officer's service dress. (Radio Times Hulton)

immediate use were bundled when the pack would prove too bulky. He is firing the famous 'knee mortar' (a misnomer – to attempt to fire it from the knee would lead to a fractured thigh) or type 89 grenade-discharger. This effective, portable weapon filled the 'range gap' between hand-grenades and conventional mortars. It had an adjustable firing mechanism, giving quite exact control of the range attained; the calibre was 50 mm., and the barrel was rifled. It could fire the Model 89 high-explosive shell, the Model 91 grenade (shown here), the Model 95 smoke shell, and several other projectiles. The Model 91 grenade was a percussion weapon; the brass cap had to be struck – usually on the side of the firer's boot – to initiate the fuse before firing.

D3 Shōsa (Major) of artillery, tropical service dress
The officers'-pattern 1938 tropical tunic was often worn with the shirt collar outside, as illustrated here. The sun helmet is the second type issued (see figure *G2*), and was of cork with a white fabric cover. The arm of service badge is worn above the breast pocket, and the rank tabs are fixed slant-wise to the lower lapels. The breeches are worn with buckled leather leggings and ankle boots. A crossbelt supports the leather holster for the Model 94 8 mm. automatic pistol.

E1 Shōshō (Major-General), 1938-pattern officer's overcoat
As stated above, by the mid-war years the field cap was worn in place of the service cap on most occasions. This ageing war-lord wears the 1938 officer's overcoat, a smart and finely cut double-breasted garment with two rows of six gilt buttons. The pockets are deeply slashed; there is a small half-belt at the back, and a slot on the left side for the sword suspenders. The rank insignia are worn on the collar in the conventional manner. The three strips of red-brown braid above the cuff identify an officer of general rank, as does the red/gold sword knot. The sword of a general would normally be of superior quality, a prized family possession.

37

E2 Infantryman, tropical field dress
In the jungle campaigns the Japanese troops frequently went into action in shirt-sleeve order; as in this case, the sleeves were sometimes hacked off short for greater ease, or for use as bandages – the Japanese Army being notoriously short of every sort of medical comfort from quite an early stage in the war. The hessian helmet cover was frequently observed, as was a scarf of some sort, often white. Pantaloon trousers, puttees and boots are conventional. This soldier, who has removed all marks of rank, is firing the crude but effective 70 mm. barrage mortar; a simple mortar tube bolted to a wooden block with a spike beneath, it was thrust into the ground at the desired angle. The shell released a number of high-explosive projectiles which fell on rice-paper parachutes. Six rounds are carried in the ammunition satchel.

E3 Jūn-i (Warrant Officer) of armoured troops
The Japanese did not make much use of their tank forces – for the excellent reasons that tanks are not naturally suited to thick jungle fighting, and that Japanese tank design lagged a decade behind that of the Allies. Nevertheless a special tank uniform was issued; it consisted of a quilted leather protective helmet, with earphone housings, and a one-piece overall suit. This Warrant Officer wears rank patches, indicating his grade on both arms (these patches seem to have been worn on left, right, both or neither arms of overalls or protective clothing of all sorts, without much regard to uniformity), and carried field-glasses in a webbing case. The crossbelt and holster for the Model 94 automatic are also moulded in rubberized fabric, which replaced leather more and more widely as the war continued; apart from the question of availability, leather had a short life in the damp jungles of South-East Asia. The Model 94, an 8 mm. weapon of poor design and workmanship, was probably the ugliest handgun ever produced, and its performance lived up to its appearance.

F1 Chū-i (1st Lieutenant), Army Air Force
This pilot is in summer flying gear; he wears a leather flying helmet, a one-piece green cotton flying suit with pile collar and zippered, slanted pockets, and leather boots with fur lining. The suit has plastic or horn buttons, and the rank patch of a company-grade officer is sewn on the arm. White silk scarves were common.

F2 Infantryman, sniper's cape
Although not outstanding shots – they were only trained up to ranges of 300 yds. – Japanese snipers were masters of camouflage, and noted for their fatalistic patience when waiting motionless in a hide for hours on end. This sniper has camouflaged his helmet with foliage attached to the hessian and netting covers, and over his mud-smeared face wears a mosquito veil of green muslin. More greenery is taped to his legs, and his split-toed *tabi* boots have climbing spikes tied on. The cape is made of coarse, feathery cotton fibres in various shades of green; it is in fact a sleeveless jerkin with an attached cape. The rifle is the 7·7 mm. Model 99 of 1939, which gradually replaced many of the Meiji 38 weapons in service during the course of the war. It was fitted with a folding monopod under the fore-end of the stock. The 4 × telescopic sights were mounted well back, with a soft rubber eyepiece; of the fixed-focus type, they gave a

A Japanese soldier captured at Changteh in Hunan Province, with his Chinese guards. He wears field service cap and the enlisted man's pattern overcoat, with hood thrown back. (Keystone)